Middle Class Philanthropist

How Anyone Can Leave a Legacy

D1623049

Middle Class Philanthropist

How Anyone Can Leave a Legacy

Melinda Gustafson Gervasi

PURPLE OWL PRESS

Middle Class Philanthropist

Copyright © 2013 by Melinda Gustafson Gervasi

ISBN 978-0-9898082-0-0

Library of Congress Control Number: 2013914858

Printed in the United States of America

First Edition

Publisher:
Purple Owl Press, LLC
Madison, Wisconsin
www.purpleowlpress.com

Email address:
info@purpleowlpress.com

Disclaimer: This book is written to provide information regarding the subject matter covered. Neither Purple Owl Press, LLC nor Melinda Gustafson Gervasi are providing legal advice, and assume no responsibility for any loss or damage incurred by anyone relying on the information within this book.

"If you can't feed a hundred people, then feed just one."

—Mother Teresa

To my children, Ian and Maeve,
who provide daily reminders of how precious life is
and the importance of planning for the future.
And for my husband Charles—
my chief champion in writing and life.

Contents

Introduction

> *"What we have done for ourselves*
> *alone, dies with us; what we have*
> *done for others and the world*
> *remains and is immortal."*
> ALBERT PIKE

In the summer of 1996, I was exploring the streets of Paris when I spotted a lovely paisley silk scarf. "Voila, this is the souvenir I should take home!" I said to my friend, a native Parisian. *"Mais non!* That store is not for us! That store is for the wealthy." Her rejection of my idea riled my inner defiant American, what do you mean not for *us?* Exclusivity has never sat well with me, yet I followed her lead and did not enter the store.

Today, as an estate planning and probate attorney, I see the same exclusivity when the topic of philanthropy enters a conversation. The prevailing belief is a philanthropic life is beyond the reach of those in the middle class. This could not be farther from the truth. It is my belief that no matter the size of your wallet, anyone can leave a legacy. As the opening quote of this book states, if you can't feed a hundred people, then feed just one. Something is far better than nothing.

Those who follow the financial newspapers know that our nation sits on the verge of the greatest inter-generational wealth transfer of all time. Estimates show that between 1998 and 2052 a total of $41 trillion will flow from the Baby Boomers, upon death, to the next generation. Imagine what our world might look like if each Baby Boomer pledged to leave ten percent of his or her assets to a charitable organization that promoted that person's life's passions and values.

Decades later, I still regret never entering that Parisian store. Not wanting another regret, I cannot keep silent on the topic of how anyone can leave a legacy. There are several wonderful books on how a typical middle-class person can be philanthropic during life, but virtually nothing on the topic of making philanthropic bequests when life ends. My goal with this book is to transform the word "philanthropy" from one believed to be reserved for high net-worth individuals and to place it solidly in the hands of America's middle class. Specifically, I want all middle-class Americans to know how one can leave a lasting legacy upon his or her death. This book will take us on a journey. As writer and reader we will:

- Explore the definition of philanthropy and philanthropist.
- Acknowledge the benefits of philanthropy beyond tax write-offs.
- Learn how to select a cause and nonprofit organization.
- Determine the type of gift.
- Learn how to make those desires legal.

Middle Class Philanthropist: How anyone can leave a legacy contains information to educate a variety of readers (but is not to be taken as legal advice). Middle-class couples with children and/or grandchildren who have spent a lifetime giving to treasured organizations may wish to give at death as a way to model behavior for the next generation. Singles with no dependents can learn how to structure a giving plan at death that nourishes causes they held dear during life. Finally, for those employed in nonprofit development offices, this piece will challenge the narrow definition too often held about who can be a philanthropist.

Philanthropy Defined

"Philanthropy flows from a loving heart,
not an overstuffed pocketbook."
DOUGLAS M. LAWSON.

Philanthropy—do images of gated estates, yachts, and complex legal documents pop into your mind? Sadly, many people believe that philanthropic behavior is limited to the likes of Andrew Carnegie, Ted Turner, Oprah Winfrey, or Bill and Melinda Gates. Upon closer examination, however, one can see that anyone, including those in the middle class, can be a philanthropist. Simply put, anyone can leave a legacy.

Predating democracy, capitalism, organized religion, and as old as humanity itself, philanthropy exists because things often go wrong, and things can always be better.[i] Defined, philanthropy is a noun meaning generous help or benevolence toward one's fellow man.[ii] Philanthropy is further defined as the effort or inclination to increase the well-being of humankind by charitable aid or donations.[iii] Primarily achieved through gifts of time and money to nonprofit organizations, philanthropic actions range from:

- Participating in a park cleanup day;
- Purchasing raffle tickets for a local nonprofit contest;
- Making an annual gift to your college alumni foundation; or
- Naming a place of worship in your will.

Nothing about these actions requires excessive amounts of money. Philanthropy only requires a desire to improve your world, not a seven-figure net worth, yet this is not a message readily shared in today's media. Far too often, news of charitable donations reads something like this "$3.6 million bequest left to art museum—largest in history!" Coverage of Bill Gates and Warren Buffett combining forces to create the world's largest philanthropic foundation made front page news.[iv] When news stories about an "average" person's charitable giving do surface, it is always in awe—how on earth could they do that? Oseola McCarty is a perfect example.

In 1908, Oseola McCarty was born to a single mother in Hattiesburg, Mississippi. Raised alongside her aunt and grandmother, she began working with her family washing clothes at age eight. In the sixth grade, she left school, never to return, in order to help make ends meet for the household. From a young age, she embraced her work with joy and reverence. Through frugal living (she never owned a car), Ms. McCarty saved her money and at age eighty-six retired with $280,000. Consulting with her banker, she signed an irrevocable trust agreement giving $150,000 of her funds to the University of Southern Mississippi to endow scholarships for needy students. This act launched her into the national media spotlight. From CNN to Life Magazine to Barbara Walter's ten most fascinating Americans of the year—Oseola McCarty's philanthropic ways made headlines.[v] While Oseola McCarty's actions make for a compelling story, she does not need to be viewed as an exception in the world of philanthropy.

Reserving philanthropy for those with a high net worth is unfortunate and incorrect. As reported in the Giving USA 2013 Annual Report on Philanthropy, in 2012, gifts to nonprofits totaled $316.23 billion. Of that number, 72 percent ($228.93 billion) were given by individuals, which stands in stark contrast to 6 percent ($18.15 billion) given by corporations and 15 percent ($45.74 billion) distributed by Foundations. The final piece of the pie, 7 percent ($23.41 billion), came from bequests at the end of life.[vi] Individuals, rich and poor, dominate giving to nonprofits.

THE CRONIN FAMILY CREATES A LEGACY

At age fifty-four, Professor Robert F. Cronin was diagnosed with Alzheimer's Disease. He died in 2001 at the age of sixty-one. He left behind a wife, two adult children, and a legacy of being a remarkable professor of rhetoric, mass communications, drama, and photography. He truly cared about the young people he helped educate at Loras College in Dubuque, Iowa. His teaching went beyond the classroom—students were invited home for dinner—they were encouraged to tackle internships and to explore all the possibilities of their degrees.

In lieu of flowers, the family received numerous donations upon his death and decided to create an endowment in Dr. Cronin's name at Loras College where he had taught for twenty-three years. The donations, combined with gifts from his widow, Rosemary, and other relatives, established the Dr. Robert F. Cronin Communication Arts Scholarship.

All it took was $15,000 for the Cronin family of Dubuque, Iowa, to become philanthropists.

Awarded once a year, the $500 scholarship is intended to make a difference in a student's life, whether it is for paying a rent bill, making a car repair, traveling to an interview, or purchasing books for a semester.

When creating an endowment, donations are placed into a fund whose sole purpose is to be invested. Using asset-allocation guidelines, the fund can be conservatively invested to guarantee an income stream. That income stream then can be used for annual distributions. In this case, income from the endowment is used to pay the annual $500 scholarship and will give in perpetuity.

Since Dr. Cronin's death, eight students, selected by the Cronin family and four faculty members, have received a scholarship. These students have joined the Cronin family for a meal or cookout, just as previous students had for decades prior to his passing. From "in lieu of flowers" donations, a devoted teacher's memory will stay alive in the lives of future students.

Would journalists write a front-page story about the Cronins? Probably not, but the Cronin family's motivations, actions, and results clearly put them in the camp of philanthropists.

Why Be Philanthropic?

> *"If you want to do something for your children and show how much you love them, the single best thing —by far—is to support organizations that will create a better world for them and their children. And by giving, we inspire others to give of themselves, whether their money or their time."*
>
> MICHAEL R. BLOOMBERG

M
r. Bloomberg, the former mayor of New York City, has a net worth exceeding $25 billion and is listed as one of the ten wealthiest persons in America. His name generates the common view of a philanthropist, however, his message extends to America's middle class: If you want a better world for your children, support organizations that you believe will bring about that world. For those without children, there are numerous other motivations to be philanthropic.

Taxes, Taxes, Taxes

Read any popular publication about planned giving and you will receive a plethora of information about the estate tax benefits of being a philanthropist. While estate taxes are likely not an issue for most of America's middle class, it is a topic one needs to know about.

Federal estate taxes are owed when the person who has died leaves a net worth that exceeds a certain limit. If the person's net worth is below the limit, the estate is considered exempt and no estate tax is owed. Note: a spouse can leave an unlimited amount to a United States citizen spouse. On January 2, 2013, President Obama signed into law the American Taxpayer Relief Act, which set the federal estate tax exemption at $5 million, retroactive to 2011, and indexed the amount for inflation. In 2013, the indexed amount was $5.25 million. This means any one person who dies can leave up to this limit and not trigger the estate tax. If triggered, a tax of up to forty percent is assessed on the amount exceeding the exemption level. Considering the amount of the current federal exemption level, the middle class most likely does not need to take steps to minimize liability. However, keep in mind that the net worth calculation includes liquid and illiquid assets and are due to the Internal Revenue Service within nine months of death. For those with cabins, businesses, or farms in the family, the federal exemption can be triggered quite quickly. A handful of states also have their own state estate tax, and one should consult with an attorney for advice.

While there are numerous approaches to limiting that estate tax liability, one relatively straightforward approach has been to include gifts to charitable organizations in a will, trust, or beneficiary form. Why? For the purposes of a federal estate tax liability calculation, assets gifted to charities are removed from the estate's net worth. For the Internal Revenue Service to recognize this gift, the organization must be a qualified 501(c)(3) organization. Also, even though worthy causes span the globe, under current law, for a gift to be considered a charitable contribution, the organization must be a United States nonprofit.

With an exemption level over $5 million, tax savings may not motivate the middle class to be philanthropic. It is the benefits beyond the tax break of giving that will motivate a new type of philanthropist.

A Gift that Keeps on Giving

Many people have a cause or causes they routinely support: weekly checks to a place of worship, monthly donation to a food bank, or participating in an annual 5k to support medical research. Your death does not have to bring an immediate end to your support of favored organizations. Plant a seed, and leave a legacy to the charitable organization you supported during life by including a final gift in your will, trust, or beneficiary forms. Even after your earthly presence is gone, your charitable gifts can continue to nurture those organizations you valued most during life.

One word of caution: reflect on the causes that mean the most to you and select those for a final gift. Listing any and all organizations that you supported during your life may result in a long list. While inclusive, giving to every organization can diminish the impact of your gift. Over the years, I have administered probates where the decedent made gifts to twenty-five or more organizations. The effect was to sprinkle a little here and a little there. This caused me to wonder what might have grown from fewer, and thus larger, final gifts to three or four organizations. For example, if there was a pot of $50,000 remaining after someone died to be distributed equally between ten organizations, each would receive $5,000. Instead, if only three organizations were named, each would receive a final gift of just over $16,600. This is a significant increase and most likely more empowering. If your list of organizations is greater than five, review and ask yourself:

- Is there one umbrella organization that addresses your desire to support the places where you have volunteered?

- Which organizations need the money the most?
- Where will your gift have the greatest potential for creating a legacy?

It Feels Good

Creating an estate plan is never a fun activity. In fact, I keep a box of chocolates in my waiting area for clients to enjoy—one deserves a little treat for tackling the question *where will it all go when I am gone?* Another way to make the experience positive is to be charitable in your estate plan. Evidence shows that charitable giving may actually make you feel good.

In 2007, an article in the journal *Science* recounted a study where people who donated money (the money had been found by the subject, perceived to have been lost by another) to a charity stimulated portions of the brain associated with pleasure.[vii] Social psychologist Sonja Lyubomirsky elaborates stating that several activities can increase ones happiness: expressing gratitude, cultivating optimism, and avoiding overthinking and social comparison.[viii] It is expressing gratitude that links charitable giving to boosting happiness.

What is an expression of gratitude? Lyubomirsky argues that expressing gratitude can be many things and goes far beyond sending a thank you note for a gift received.[ix] In her book, *The How of Happiness,* she defines the practice of gratitude as "a focus on the present moment, on appreciating your life as it is today and what has made it so."[x]

Why does expressing gratitude boost happiness? In *The How of Happiness,* Lyubomirsky lists eight reasons grateful living makes a person happier, it:

- Promotes savoring positive life experiences;
- Allows you to feel more confident by realizing how much others have done for you and what you have accomplished;
- Helps one cope with stress and trauma;
- Encourages moral and kind behavior;
- Strengthens existing social bonds and nurtures new ones;
- Reduces envy because you are less inclined to compare your accomplishments to others; and
- Prevents you from taking the good things in life for granted.[xi]

Lyubomirsky's definition is well suited for the act of being charitable in a will. Facing your own mortality grounds you in the present moment. Assessing where you are in the present allows you to appreciate life today and how you got there. And finally, reflecting on how you got to the present can reveal what and who assisted you along the way. Does a nonprofit organization come to mind when practicing gratitude? If so, could it become a recipient under your estate planning documents?

Set an Example For The Next Generation

Anyone with children, especially young children, knows that the youth of society learn by example. This is painfully clear when words, expressions, or tones flow from the mouth of child and the parent turns bright red. It seems that all parents have lighthearted stories in which a small child used a word or phrase normally reserved for adults because they were parroting a parent's behavior. However, the influential effects of a parent's actions do not necessarily end when the child enters adulthood. One can set an example throughout life and at its end. If you are charitable at the end of your life, chances are your children will be as well.

Make The World a Better Place

We often view charitable giving from the viewpoint of the giver. From tax breaks to boosting happiness to setting an example for their own children, the focus is on the giftor. Yet charitable giving greatly impacts our larger society.

There are the obvious receivers in charitable giving. For example, there are direct recipients—such as homeowners receiving care packages after a fire. More broadly, we are all indirect recipients of the charitable actions of others, past and present.[xii] Philanthropic giving benefits social change, stewardship, and the advancement of knowledge. Everyone benefits from those actions, as exemplified by public libraries. Even if you do not have a library card, they provide a service that improves the quality of life for all in the community by providing free computer use for job seekers and books for low-income children.[xiii]

Currently, we are in the midst of the greatest intergenerational transfer of wealth ever seen. Between 1998 and 2052, an estimated $41 trillion will flow from the estates of Baby Boomers to their heirs.[xiv] Imagine the impact on social change, stewardship, and the advancement of knowledge if just ten percent of that $41 trillion passed charitably. When you do the math, it comes out to $4.1 trillion if only ten percent were earmarked for that purpose. That is nearly half the annual economic output of the entire United States economy. Just think what 10 percent could do!

The Ease Factor

Look around you. Are you surrounded by stuff, material goods? Most likely the answer is yes, to varying degrees. And what will happen to all of those items when you pass? In the world of estate planning professionals we call it your TPP, which stands for Tangible Personal Property. Everything from jewelry to collectables to furniture to hobbyist equipment. And my oh my, it can cause enormous family disputes, some so severe the damage will never be undone. Even if your TPP would not cause a family feud, it still raises the question— what to do with it all? Directing it to charity is one way to ease the tension and workload on the loved ones you leave behind. For example:

- Include a clause in your will that directs your TPP to be sold at a public garage sale, with all proceeds benefiting your favorite cause, such as the local animal shelter.
- Easier yet, direct that specific items be donated directly to a charity. For example, a life's collection of books can be donated to support a local library book sale.
- Donate a vehicle to a nonprofit to be auctioned off to raise funds to support research related to curing an illness you battled.
- Old photographs may benefit a local historical society.
- Furniture can be given to nonprofits working with displaced families who are setting up a home.
- Kitchen equipment can be left to a domestic abuse shelter.

JANE BURROWS BUFFETT, BETTY CUSTER HARRIS, AND THE SNOWBALL EFFECT

Already a teacher, wife, and mother, Jane Burrows Buffett embarked on a legal education. Earning her law degree from the University of Wisconsin-Madison, she went on to become a labor mediator for the State of Wisconsin. She was also very active in her community. It was through her church that she became involved with the Wexford Ridge Community Center—an organization that would greatly benefit from Jane's energy and passion.

Over time Jane's involvement with the center grew. It became obvious that its space, a unit in an apartment complex, was far too small. A larger space was needed—and Jane wanted to see this need met. During this time frame, through a routine blood test, Jane learned she had multiple myeloma, then an always fatal disease. Turning pain into inspiration, Jane and her husband Roger decided that a large portion of her state employee retirement account should be designated to the community center she helped found. Upon her death in 2004, the Wexford Ridge Community Center received approximately $75,000 from her retirement account.

Jane's earthly time may have come to an end before a new building was established, but her passion for a community center continued on. Her gift of $75,000 sparked a capital campaign charged with raising $4.5 million to build a new building for the center. It was her dear friend Betty Harris Custer who stepped into the shoes Jane left—"I knew she would chair the campaign if she were here. I had no other choice." said Betty. After countless meetings, relentless phone calls, and three years, the $4.5 million was secured, and the Lussier Center was born. Housed on land associated with James Madison Memorial High School in Madison, Wisconsin, the Lussier Center offers many programs, including an endowment fund (funded by the initial $4.5 million capital campaign) to help students who want to become the first generation in their family to attend college. The fund supports college test preparation classes and other efforts to help determined students stay on track. Nearly two decades before its inception, I graduated from that very high school. Not unlike students today, I was the first generation in my family to seek a college degree. Back then no support system existed. But thanks to the inspiration of Jane Burrows Buffett and the determination of Betty Harris Custer, a college education is more achievable for James Madison Memorial students. All it took was passion, drive, and a portion of a state retirement fund.

Nonprofits—
The What and How

"To give away money is an easy matter and in any man's power. But to decide to whom to give it and how large and when, and for what purpose and how, is neither in every man's power nor an easy matter."

ARISTOTLE

M y reply to Aristotle would take the form of two objections. First, I would substitute the word "person" in place of "man". And second, every contemporary American does have the power to decide what goes where. I agree that it is not an easy matter, but it is a very important one. Motivated to give but uncertain where to direct your gifts? You are not alone, and you are not without help. Navigating the process of selecting a cause or causes requires three steps. First, learn more about what exactly is a nonprofit. Second, examine how to select an organization that meshes with your values. And third, name an organization that will put your gift to the best use.

What Is a Nonprofit?

America's charitable roots extend back to colonial times and offer twin approaches. One comes from the Christian spirit of charity, and the other stems from a secular spirit of voluntarism.[xv] Over a span of seventy-five years, from 1894 to 1969, the United States Congress created the body of law governing America's nonprofit sector. The Tariff Act of 1894 stated that charitable organizations were exempt from federal income taxes. In 1917, the concept of an individual receiving an income tax deduction for charitable donations was introduced. The next year, charitable deductions for the estate tax were created. The Revenue Act of 1954 created the modern tax code, with the reference to section 501(c), and placed limits on political activities of nonprofits.[xvi]

Today, review by the Internal Revenue Service is required when an organization desires to become a nonprofit. Current regulations to qualify for tax-exempt status require the organization to show its purpose is to serve the public good, as opposed to a private interest. For example, purposes may range from religious to scientific to literary or educational pursuits.[xvii] The current tax code recognizes twenty-eight types of nonprofit organizations. Nonprofits range in size and structure, including a corporation, trust, association, cooperative, or other organizational form. Unlike a business, making a profit is not the primary focus of charitable organizations. Instead, a nonprofit organization operates primarily for scientific, educational, service, charitable, or similar purposes in the public interest. Net proceeds are used to maintain, improve, or expand operations of the organization.[xviii] Organizations granted tax-exempt status have limited ability to lobby or be politically active. Once officially classified as a 501(c)(3) organization under the Internal Revenue Code, the nonprofit may receive contributions that are tax deductible to the donee.

Finding a nonprofit to include in your estate plan can be a challenge because of the sheer volume of organizations. In 2011, there were 1.08 million tax exempt organizations registered with the Internal Revenue Service.[xix] While some people have a standard go-to list of causes important to them, others may need to do some digging. When approaching the question of where to be philanthropic, I urge you to focus more on *what you can accomplish* rather than *how much* you can give.

What Is Important To You?

The selection of the right nonprofit stems from what you value most. I direct a large portion of my charitable work and giving to the American Heart Association for one simple reason: but for pacemaker technology, my mother would have died the summer of 2008, weeks before my first child was born. I know that the time and money I put towards the American Heart Association will fund cardiac research and education, without which my children would never have known their grandmother. Nearly everyone has some giving experience rooted in their culture, faith, personal belief system, or family tree.[xx]

When answering this question, begin by identifying a cause or causes that are near and dear to your heart. Here are a few questions which may lead you in the right direction:

- Which nonprofits do you currently support with monetary donations?
- Where do you donate your time?
- Have there been organizations that played a pivotal role in your life, for example, your college?
- Have you received help or assistance from an organization at a prior time in your life that made a huge difference?
- What is wrong in the world?
- What is broken that needs to be fixed?
- What matters the most in the world?
- What keeps you up at night?
- What gets you out of bed in the morning?[xxi]

Match Your Cause To An Organization

When attempting to isolate one nonprofit from the 1.08 million recognized by the Internal Revenue Service, it may help to place the cause dear to your heart inside one of the nine categories as used in the Giving USA Annual report. Doing so overlays a structure on your passions:

- Religion
- Education
- Foundations
- Human Services
- Health
- Public-Society Benefit
- Arts, Culture, and Humanities
- International Affairs
- Environment or Animals[xxii]

Other things to consider when matching your passions with an organization include the fact that donations can be made directly to an organization, such as the local humane society, or indirectly via an intermediary agency, such as the United Way. Finally, consider whether the nonprofit has a local, state, or national office. If so, which one would you prefer to support?

Evaluate Your Selection

Once you have found some organizations that pique your interest, you should plan to spend a little time evaluating the nonprofit candidates you have found. Before naming an organization in your estate plan, take some time to ensure your gift will actually achieve your desired goals. Caution—the nonprofit sector is not exempt from blatant acts of fraud. There are numerous examples of frauds in which an entity selects a name similar to a well-known organization, so that it can siphon off donations. Less egregious are legitimate nonprofits that simply lack sound fiscal practices and/or fail to achieve stated goals. Before naming an organization, do a bit of homework first.

Deciding on what makes a charity "good" varies from person to person. However, key characteristics will include: providing bona fide programs, exercising fiscal responsibility, measuring the impact of its programs, and fulfilling its mission. When assessing a nonprofit on your own, consider utilizing the following tools mentioned by The Federal Trade Commission, the nation's consumer protection agency:[xxiii]

- If possible, make an in-person visit to the organization so that you can observe and ask questions of its staff. Before going, develop some who, what, why, and when questions.

- Utilize the website Charity Navigator, to evaluate the financial health of over 5,000 nonprofits (www.charitynavigator.org).
- Visit the website GuideStar, a nonprofit itself that aims to bring greater transparency to the evaluation of nonprofits by providing a database with information on more than one million nonprofits. Users can run reports comparing nonprofits in several areas, including salary compensation, as well as confirm a nonprofit's charitable status (www.guidestar.org).
- Contact your State Attorney General Office to see if they maintain a lists of registered nonprofits and investigate complaints of fraud and abuse.
- Check with the Internal Revenue Service to ensure that the nonprofit complies with tax exempt requirements (www.irs.gov/charities).
- Contact the American Institute of Philanthropy, which evaluates the financial health of large United States nonprofits (www.charitywatch.org).
- Contact the Better Business Bureau's Wise Giving Alliance, which focuses on business practices, such as governance and regulatory compliance (www.bbb.org/us/charity).
- Evaluate annual reports from the organization related to its mission achievements. Determine

if the organization knows where and why it has made progress.

- Ask how much of a donation goes to program services versus overhead costs. However, keep in mind that low overhead does not necessarily translate into good results. Investing in excellent staff may be far more important. As noted by other scholars, many nonprofits use volunteers to achieve goals, skewing administrative costs higher when viewed as a percentage of expenditures.[xxiv]

EMPOWERING THE SEWING MACHINE PROJECT

Do you want a relatively small amount of money to make a big impact? If yes, consider grassroots organizations—where a little can go a long way.

In 2005, Margaret Jankowski read a BBC article covering how the December 2004 Southeast Asia tsunami swept away a woman's sewing machine, one she had saved for years to purchase. Gone was not only a machine, but the woman's livelihood as well. Inspired, Margaret founded The Sewing Machine Project. An avid sewer herself, she began collecting new and old sewing machines to ship to the devastated region. In September of 2005, efforts shifted gears to assist sewers in the New Orleans region following its devastating hurricane. The machines she sent not only helped rebuild lives but created sewing based businesses.

In the spring of 2010, a recent Illinois widower found himself with a sewing room left behind after his wife's passing. It was full of sewing items gathered from years of traveling around the world—fabric, notions, and more. Wanting to ease his pain, he contacted the Sewing Machine Project to come clean out the room and put the materials to good use. Margaret realized that this same scenario plays out each day in the world. Every day sewers depart, leaving behind lovely and useful materials. Included in the sewing room supplies were lovely handmade labels; sewers commonly include a personalized label on finished products as a way to autograph or sign a piece. The labels left behind were embroidered with a Forget Me Not flower. Tucked away, those Forget Me Not flower labels would provide inspiration for yet another program.

Momentum continued to build at the Sewing Machine Project. In the fall of 2010, an influx of checks began to arrive in its mailbox. Most included some small reference to the memory of "Viola", an unknown woman to the members of The Sewing Machine Project. Who was she? Curious, Margaret went online to search and found an obituary for a woman named Viola Kraemer. The announcement ended with a suggestion to donate money in lieu of flowers to The Sewing Machine Project. Her family did some internet research upon her death and found The Sewing Machine Project. While Viola did not have a connection to the organization in her life, it mirrored her passion for sewing and was a small grassroots organization the family assumed would benefit from donations. In total the donations sent in Viola's memory represented ten percent of its annual operating budget, a very welcome bump. Over the years many of those donors continue to send in small donations, $10 here and $35 there, as a way to remember the passion of a dear friend.

As the influence of Viola Kraemer settled over the organization, Margaret remembered the labels donated from the Illinois widower. Inspiration hit, and the Forget Me Not program was born. Now, through the Forget Me Not program, loved ones can donate sewing supplies to be redistributed along with sewing machines.

If your assets are modest, you can still create a wave of positive influence by contributing to a grassroots nonprofit. As seen with The Sewing Machine Project, items such as machines, tools, and materials can be distributed to those in need. And monies in lieu of flowers, when combined, represent a substantial portion of a grassroots organization's budget.

Make it Legal

"Your estate plan is more than dry legal documentation. Your estate plan is a testament to who you are and what you love. Make sure your estate plan reflects what is most important in your life so that your plan truly becomes your lasting legacy."
TRACY GARY

For most people, the actual act of creating or updating an estate plan ranks somewhere between elective root canal surgery and attending an Internal Revenue Service audit hearing. There are people who actually enjoy putting their affairs in order (primarily off-the-chart Type A's). In reality, most people would rather put off this part of leaving a legacy for another day. Should you fall into this category, one word can help you to muster the inspiration you need to forge ahead. That word is "control". If you do not put your wishes into a legally binding format, they will likely never materialize.

Sitting down to update or create an estate plan means you are taking control of what happens to your assets (and minor children if you have them) when you die. Without a plan, assets will pass according to state statute, a pattern you may or may not agree with. So, pour something good to drink and keep reading. Please remember, a book is no substitute for legal advice given by an attorney. Books inspire, provide education, and look great stacked on the coffee table. Books cannot address the legal specifications, which vary from state to state and tend to change over time.

Questioning the necessity of an estate plan is something I hear all the time from people "What do I need an estate plan for?—I am not a Kennedy or Rockefeller." My answer is simple: anyone over 18 needs an estate plan. It may not look exactly like the Kennedy or Rockefeller estate plan, but they all share three key points: planning for illness, death, and taxes. Within those papers you can plant the seeds of your plan to leave a legacy, no matter its size and scope.

Once a plan to leave a legacy takes shape in your mind, it is time to put that plan on paper, legal paper. Remember, your charitable giving can occur during life and at death.

Making something legal involves a few steps:

- Figure out what you own.
- Determine if federal and/or state estate taxes are a concern.
- Decide what person(s) and/or organizations should inherit assets.
- Think about contingencies.
- Create the legal paperwork.
- Hire an attorney when needed.

What do you own?

When developing an estate plan you need an understanding of the types of property you own; probate and/or non-probate. Probate property is property that has no clear direction of who should receive it upon your death. When you die the court reviews your will to see who should receive any probate property. If you have no will, then the court distributes the property according to statutory guidelines. Typical examples of probate property include, but are not limited to, your home, real estate, jewelry, your car, or bank accounts. In contrast, you also likely own non-probate property. This is property that has a clear direction of who should receive it upon your death; it has a label stating where it should go. Because this property passes according to the label it passes OUTSIDE of your will and is not subject to court oversight for disposition. Examples of non-probate property include, but are not limited to, life insurance, retirement accounts, annuities, and any accounts with a "pay on death" or "transfer on death" card, and living trusts.

Wrapping your head around what type of property you own is central to developing a sound plan for what happens to your assets after you are gone. If you are a visual learner, create a chart or list. Begin by naming all of the assets you own. Second, you need to check off whether they have a label, making them non-probate, or whether they are probate, meaning your will or state statute will control distribution. Labels for non-probate assets can be hard to recognize, but here are the most common types:

- Completed beneficiary form on life insurance;
- Completed beneficiary form on retirement accounts;
- Transfer on Death card (TOD) on bank or credit union accounts;
- Pay on Death card (POD) on brokerage accounts;
- Phrase "joint tenancy" on titles or deeds (house, car, bank accounts);
- Phrase "marital property with the right to survivorship" on titles or deeds;
- Asset in the name of a living trust (i.e. deed to the home states The Melinda Gustafson Gervasi Living Trust, November 18, 2010); and

- Home has a Transfer on Death deed with a named beneficiary.

Are Federal and/or State Estate Taxes a Concern?

Central to this question is the issue of the "exemption level," a term used to describe the asset level at which an estate tax is first applied. Estates below the level are exempt, while estates above are subject to the tax.

In 2013, the estate tax is $5.25 million per person (married couples can pass an unlimited amount to a surviving spouse who is a US citizen). That number changes each year as it is indexed to inflation. Most people hear this number and quickly dismiss the chance that they will die with an estate large enough to trigger the tax. While that is probably true, it would be wise to give the question two minutes of your time—net worth that exceeds the exemption level is taxed at approximately 40 percent. Add up the value of all that you own: home, retirement accounts, investments, life insurance. Yes, I wrote life insurance. If you own the policy, its value will most likely be included in the calculation of the federal estate tax. This fact throws many people off because of differences between thinking about income tax and estate tax. The proceeds from a life insurance payout are not included in the named beneficiary's income tax return. For estate tax purposes, however, the sum is included in your estate if you die. For those with hefty policies, a consultation with an attorney and/or accountant is prudent. In addition to the federal estate tax, some states may implement their own estate tax.

Who Do You Want To Help After You Are Gone?

Most people have an obvious answer to this question. Those married with children nearly always say, to my spouse and then to my children. If your family structure does not yield an obvious answer, pose the question, "Who depends on me?" Might it be an elderly parent, a sibling, a pet, or do you fill a vital role at a nonprofit? Posing the question "Where do I want my assets to go when I die?" is not a pleasant one, but if you do not plan, then you have no control over the situation—state statute will take it out of your hands, and it may or may not be a distribution plan you agree with. For example, if you die with no surviving spouse, children, or parents, your disabled sister may inherit under state statute, which may jeopardize her government benefits.

Have a Contingency Plan

If the person or persons you named above predecease you or die at the same time, where should the assets go? Again, without creating a plan for your assets, state statute will control. A thorough estate plan will consider contingencies for every person listed. For example, *if my spouse predeceases me, then to my children. If I have no children, then to any grandchildren.* As an estate planning attorney, I encourage clients to include a nonprofit in their plan for one simple reason, organizations do not die. They may change names, or merge, but generally nonprofit charters require them to transfer remaining funds to a similar cause if they become defunct.

If you want to include a nonprofit in your estate plan, it is essential to list the organization(s) properly. This should include the organization's complete legal name, federal tax ID number, as well as the city and state where it is headquartered. Sadly, legal disputes develop between national and local chapters of nonprofits when a designation is not specific as to which entity should be the recipient. For example, an Ohio resident named six charities on his IRA beneficiary form. One of the six simply said "Alzheimer's Research Center," which was not an official name of any organization. Three different organizations stepped forward to claim the distribution. Two had received donations from the individual while he was living, and the third was a local organization with no apparent connection to the man, but contained the three words Alzheimer's Research

Center in its name. Ultimately, the monies were split between the three different organizations.[xxv] Keeping this in mind, contact the organization to obtain:

- The organization's full and complete legal name (i.e. Inc., Foundation, etc.);
- Its address, city, and state;
- Its federal EIN number (tax number issued by the Internal Revenue Service); and
- A phrase including "its legal successor organization" should the entity adjust or modify its name in the future.

Routinely clients will ask *"Can I leave my car to my sister and the rest of my estate to my two adult children?"* Yes. Remember, creating an estate plan is about taking control of the situation. You can basically do as you please when creating an estate plan, as long as you are not violating public policy. For example, it is considered a violation of public policy to write a will saying "my entire estate goes to my son, but only if he divorces his wife" because encouraging divorce is considered to be against public policy.

A common question posed during my work with clients is, "If I die tomorrow, before this is signed, is it binding?" No. Procrastination is not wise in the area of estate planning. We all know we are going to die; we just have no idea when. Without the proper papers in place, your wishes and intent may never be realized. At this time it is important to refer back to the section on probate versus non-probate property. Remember, probate property is distributed based on the directions in a will. Non-probate property is distributed according to beneficiary forms. Determine what will be distributed via your will and what will be distributed by one of the various non-probate beneficiary formats.

Wills Accomplish Several Things

Wills nominate who should be in charge of the probate process; state where your property should go; and if you have minor children, nominate a guardian. Common ways to include a nonprofit in your will include:

- I leave $1,000 to Charity X.
- I leave ten percent of the residue (which is what remains of your probate estate after final bills, taxes, and expenses have been paid) to Charity Y.
- I leave any automobile I own at the time of my death to Charity Z.

Practically, leaving a percentage of your estate to a nonprofit is preferable to a dollar amount because one never knows what final amount will be left to distribute. Depending on the amount that remains, a specific dollar amount may constitute a larger or smaller percentage than desired. Leaving $5,000 of $30,000 is a much larger percentage than $5,000 out of $950,000. Moreover, writing in a dollar amount today will diminish over time simply because of inflation—$5,000 will be worth far less in 2046. Finally, if you already have a will, keep in mind that it is possible to add a charitable donation through an amendment called a codicil. A new will is not necessarily needed. For example, if your will currently states "everything to my sister," you could create an amendment saying "half to my sister and half to the local animal shelter." An amendment to a will needs to be executed in the same manner as a will. Requirements are state specific, and it is wise to consult an attorney in your state for procedures, rather than simply crossing out lines and making handwritten modifications.

Wills are not always well-received in society. Some people go to great lengths to avoid them. Why? First, there is the cost of probate. A percentage of the net value of probate property (assets minus any liens) is subject to a fee, payable to the court. Fees range greatly from state to state. In my home state of Wisconsin, the fee is relatively small—0.2 percent. However, in other states it can be as high as 10 or 12 percent. Direct transfers, such as beneficiary forms on retirement funds, avoid the probate process and are not subject to this fee. Second, there is the time. The process to transfer assets from the decedent to the beneficiary takes time, often twelve to eighteen months or more. Direct transfers via a beneficiary form happen almost immediately. And third, there are the dreaded legal fees. Depending on your situation you may need to hire an attorney to draft or amend your will, costing hundreds to thousands of dollars beyond the gift you wish to make.

For those reasons, the area of non-probate transfers has grown. Conducted outside of the probate court, most non-probate transfers require submission of a form stating the owner has died, contact information for the listed beneficiaries, and a death certificate. Varied in scope and complexity, means of non-probate transfer offer attractive alternatives for distributing assets upon death. What follows is a brief discussion of each device and how it could include a nonprofit in your estate plan. I will begin with the less complicated methods.

Bank or Brokerage Accounts

Including a nonprofit in your estate plan may be as simple as filling out a card at your bank, credit union, or brokerage. POD Cards (Pay-On-Death) at banks and credit unions or TODs (Transfer-On-Death) at brokerages allow you to name a primary or secondary beneficiary for the account. It can be a quick and simple way to leave laddered CDs to your favorite nonprofit.

Life Insurance Policies

If you have a current life insurance policy, you could name a charitable organization as either a primary, secondary, or final beneficiary. Another option is to purchase a new policy with a charitable organization named as the beneficiary. You would pay the premiums now, with the gift being paid upon your death.

Retirement Accounts

If you own a 401(k), IRA, 403(b), etc., you have the option of listing a charitable organization as a primary or secondary beneficiary. For example, you may wish to leave ten percent to Charity Y. Or, you may wish to say, "The primary beneficiary is my spouse. If my spouse predeceases me, then the beneficiary is Charity Z." If tax efficiency is a motivator for you, investigate the benefits of leaving tax-deferred retirement accounts to nonprofits. Retirement accounts left to individuals will be subject to an income tax when paid out, but those same dollars avoid income taxes when left to qualified 501(c)(3) organizations.

Charitable Gift Annuity

A charitable gift annuity is a contract between you and

a charitable organization. You agree to make a gift to the charity and in return, the charity agrees to make income payments to you for the rest of your life. Check with the charitable organization to see if they offer this option.

Donor-Advised Funds

Does the idea of a foundation appeal to you, but you do not have a few million dollars for its creation? If so, consider either a public or community foundation, which allows individuals to create charitable funds akin to a large foundation. Because they serve many people and causes, they can pool resources and keep the administration costs low. Each fund has its own specific purpose or focus. Donor-advised funds can be established through community foundations (such as the Madison Community Foundation), financial institutions (like Vanguard Charitable), and public charities (such as hospitals). If you are considering using a donor-advised fund, several things you should consider include:

- What are the minimum funding requirements?
- What assets will they accept (cash, cars, homes, stocks)?
- How many generations of successors are allowed?
- What is the frequency of grants being made

(annually, quarterly)? What services are offered (research, meetings, etc.)?

- What fee does the foundation charge?

Living Trusts

A living trust is a legal document that both aims to avoid probate as well as to create a vehicle to hold and control assets. Living trusts are created during a person's lifetime, into which assets are transferred (called funding). Assets are transferred to the trust by a grantor or grantors—essentially the person or persons who owned property. Once assets are transferred, the assets are managed by a "trustee" for beneficiaries. Typically a married couple would be the grantors, trustees, and beneficiaries. Because the trust document contains a distribution plan for the trust assets upon the death of one or both of the grantors, assets held in the name of the trust are considered to be non-probate property. This means any property titled in the name of the trust is not distributed according to a will, but rather by the plan in the trust document. A trust agreement can distribute some or all assets to a nonprofit as a primary and/or secondary beneficiary. For example:

- Upon the death of both spouses, the remaining trust assets shall be divided into three equal shares and distributed as follows: one share to our son, one share to our daughter, and one share to Charity Z.

Charitable Remainder Trusts

These vehicles allow you to transfer ownership of property you have to that of the trust. Instead of it being owned by you, it would be owned by the trust. With charitable remainder trusts, you can be a beneficiary now, and upon your death the remaining balance is paid to the charitable organization. These instruments are commonly used by people who have held mutual funds, stocks, or real estate for a long period of time because of tax advantages of leaving highly appreciated assets to a nonprofit organization.

Hiring an Attorney

Creating an estate plan does not require working with a professional who wears a pin-striped suit and sits behind a mahogany desk with an expensive view of the cityscape. Yes, a visit to a lawyer's office may be needed, or maybe not, but keep in mind there are attorneys who shun the suits and fancy trappings as much as you do. My tips for finding a quality, yet down-to-earth, attorney include:

- Ask friends and family if they had legal help with a will or powers of attorney. If so, they either love them or hate them, and will gladly tell you about the experience.

- Get a referral from your CPA, financial planner, insurance agent, or banker. If you like that person's style, they may know of an attorney who operates the same way.

- Interview three to four attorneys. Yes, interview them. They will be working for you, so take the time to get to know them first. If they are unwilling to talk briefly or are not forthcoming, move on. Keep in mind that to get gold-star legal advice you must be willing to disclose information related to family structure and finances. You have to open up to this person, so make sure your personalities align. In the course of my practice I have had clients share very private aspects of their life, including giving up children for adoption in high school. Planning can be emotional. Make sure you are comfortable enough to trust this person with information about your finances, family structure, and legacy aspirations. Excellent legal advice depends on the lawyer having in-depth knowledge of the client's life. Without details, a lawyer cannot give sound legal advice.

- Find an attorney who focuses on estate planning and probate. Sure, your cousin may have a bankruptcy practice and be willing to give you a family discount. But first ask yourself, would you have your allergist perform your c-section? Most likely not. Focus areas mean the attorney should have precise and in-depth knowledge of wills, powers of attorney, and probate. Generalists run the risk of spreading their knowledge too thin.

- Opt for a flat-fee attorney instead of one with an hourly rate. This means you will be less likely to keep looking at your watch, wondering how much will this cost, allowing you to thoroughly interact with your attorney.

- Check out the attorney with the regulatory agency. This will be state specific. Some regulatory or professional associations merely collect dues and require attorneys to sit through continuing legal education. You want to check out the attorney with the licensing entity to find out if other clients have filed complaints. Sadly, it is not unheard of for attorneys to steal from client funds or show up drunk to court. Investigate if you can.

- Get it in writing. Request that the attorney put the terms of service in writing – how do they charge (flat-fee, hourly, etc.), what do they charge, what services are offered, what services are not offered (I, for example, do not complete tax returns for clients because I am not a CPA). Some states may require this information, called an engagement letter or legal services agreement, and others may not. Either way, getting the terms on paper is smart before hiring an attorney.

GAIL SHEFFIELD—CHAMPION OF FERAL CATS IN LIFE AND IN DEATH

Gail Sheffield's four-paged, handwritten will left her entire estate to two organizations where she had been highly involved during her life. Following her death, after a short illness, those bequests are still making a huge difference in the world of feral cats.

In her will, Ms. Sheffield left her home to the Flathead Spay & Neuter Task Force, a one-of-a-kind organization in Montana. According to the organization's director, Mimi Beadles, the organization sold the home and received $290,000 – an amount equivalent to three years of revenue! As a result of the bequest, the burden of fundraising has been lessened. The bequest ensures the financial stability of the organization for years to come. Moreover, according to Ms. Beadles, the rainy day fund that was created from the bequest allows volunteers to focus on the grueling work of capturing, treating, and releasing feral cats. Gail Sheffield's gift of her home amplified efforts in the field, allowing the true mission of the organization to thrive. In her honor, the building that houses Flathead Spay & Neuter Task Force has been renamed the Gail Sheffield Memorial Clinic.

Gail Sheffield's will also left a bequest to another nonprofit with a similar mission. Her will left $100,000 to the Feral Cat Consortium in Madisonville, Louisiana, a dollar amount that represents about three years of its annual operating expenses. A portion of the bequest is being used to trap and release feral cats in the New Orleans area, continuing Gail's own efforts as a volunteer in the field. Since January of 2013 over 300 cats have been trapped, spayed or neutered, and released. The remaining portion has gone to support the general missions of the Feral Cat Consortium, which aims to reduce feral cat colonies through attrition due to spay and neuter, and to manage problem behavior of the feral cat colonies through detractors and feeding programs to draw the animals away from homes. As an all-volunteer organization, its director, Wendy Guidry, emphasized that the gift was far more than an infusion of cash: "It was a concrete, gigantic thank-you for thankless work on a seemingly endless problem." Her gift not only gave the organization operating dollars but empowered volunteers to be more aggressive in project ideas. It allowed volunteers to work harder because the limitation of no funding was no longer a boundary.

Conclusion

"If there's a book you really want to read, but it hasn't been written yet, then you must write it."
TONI MORRISON

n her book, *The How of Happiness: A New Approach to Getting the Life You Want,* Sonja Lyubomirsky writes that we live in a world that reinforces "saying no." When we avoid "saying yes" at all costs, we are limiting ourselves and potentially our happiness. "The deed need not be grand or complicated." [xxvi]

As we, author and reader, approach the end of this writing, I urge you to say "yes" and embrace philanthropy in your will or other end-of-life planning documents. In closing, I will leave you with some of my favorite ways for the middle class to be philanthropic at death:

- Direct "in lieu of flowers" memorials to a nonprofit. During my research I read a moving story of a woman who was in hospice care and overheard her daughters discussing making a contribution to a research foundation related to her disease. She called her daughters in and said, "No, I want you to figure out a way to honor what I valued in life, not the disease the ended my life." As a result, with modest donations, the library where she had volunteered was able to purchase books for the children's section.[xxvii]

- Leave instructions in your will to have all of your household items sold at a garage sale, with the proceeds going to a nonprofit. Go further and instruct that the sellers promote this gesture at the sale (i.e., yard signs stating proceeds will support the local animal shelter).

- If you have an item that no loved one wants or would enjoy, consider leaving it to a charity to auction off. A previous client of mine owned a Model-T car, but neither his wife nor children shared his passion for the vehicle. Instead, he directed it to a charity for auction.

- Do you have a small checking or savings account you use for travel or holiday purchases? If so, consider putting a pay-on-death card on the account, leaving it to a nonprofit.

- Is there a pile of old photographs, clothing, dishes, etc., growing in your attic or basement?

Consider whether an historical society would benefit from a contribution.

During my research I found the quote by Toni Morrison and have replayed it in my mind as I worked to mold the idea of this book into an actual volume for readers. Middle-class people who want to be generous can choose from several titles if their focus is on how to volunteer their time during life. People with millions to give away in grants or to establish a family foundation have a plethora of resources to guide them. However, from what I can tell, there is no inspirational handbook available for middle-class people that want to leave a legacy upon their death. A void exists, and I had to fill it.

The wonder of the digital age is the ability to continue a conversation long after the last page in a book is written. Do you have a story to share, question to raise, or comment to offer? If so, please visit www.purpleowlpress. com. Death does not mean the middle class must stop giving. Anyone can plant the seeds of a legacy. A little, given in just the right way, can create wonderful results.

"Everyone—regardless of income, available time, age, and skills—can do something useful for others and, in the process, strengthen the fabric of our shared humanity."
—President Bill Clinton

Glossary of Terms

Beneficiary is the person who receives part of a decedent's estate through a will, trust, life insurance or retirement proceeds.

Codicil is an amendment to your will.

Decedent is a person who has died.

Estate is the decedent's property.

Fiduciary is one who holds something in trust for another, such as a trustee.

Heir is a person who inherits property.

Intangible personal property represented by an instrument, such as a stock certificate.

Intestacy means having died without a will.

Issue are offspring, such as children or grandchildren.

Joint tenancy means title to property held in two

or more names, upon death of one owner, his or her interest automatically passes to the others.

Marital property refers to assets acquired during marriage.

Non-probate property is property not subject to probate, such as life insurance or retirement benefits. This type of property passes according to written beneficiary designations, and not via a will.

Pay-on-Death card. Commonly called a POD, it is a type of beneficiary form you can put on bank or credit union accounts, converting them to non-probate property.

Personal representative is the person or corporate representative appointed by a will or court to administer the decedent's estate through probate; commonly called the executor.

Power of attorney is the legal right to act on another's behalf.

Probate is the court proceeding during which ownership of a decedent's property is transferred and taxes and bills are paid.

Probate property is property that is distributed via a will, such as cars, jewelry, or other tangible items.

Tangible property is property that itself has value.

Tenancy-in-common is when title is held in two or more names, and when one person dies, his or her interest passes via will or statutory designation.

Testamentary trust is a trust created by a will.

Transfer-On-Death card. Commonly called a TOD, it is a beneficiary form you can use with brokerage accounts to convert them to non-probate property.

Trust is a form of property ownership where title is held by a trustee who has a duty to manage the trust for the benefit of beneficiaries.

Will is a legal statement directing the distribution of the decedent's probate property at death.

Bibliography

Anik, Lain, et al. "Feeling Good About Giving: The Benefits and Costs of Self-Interested Charitable Behavior." Working Paper. Harvard Business School. 2009.

Arnold, Elizabeth. *Creating the Good Will: The Most Comprehensive Guide to Both the Financial AND Emotional Sides of Passing On Your Legacy.* New York: Penguin Group, 2005.

Arnsberger, Paul, et al. "A History of the Tax-Exempt Sector: An SOI Perspective." Internal Revenue Service. Winter 2007-2008.

Clinton, Bill. *Giving: How Each Of Us Can Change The World.* New York: Alfred A. Knopf, 2007.

Friedman, Lawrence J. and Mark D. McGravie. Charity, Philanthropy, and Civility in American History. Cambridge: University Press, 2003.

Fullwood, Valaida. *Giving Back: A Tribute to Generations of African American Philanthropists.* Charlotte, North Carolina: Foundation for the Carolinas, 2011.

Federal Trade Commission. "Consumer

Information: Before Giving to a Charity." June 2012 http://www.consumer.ftc.gov/articles/0074-giving-charity.

Gary, Tracy. *Inspired Philanthropy: Your Step-to-Step Guide to Creating A Giving Plan and Leaving a Legacy.* San Francisco: Jossey-Bass, 2008.

Giving USA. *Giving USA 2012 Annual Report.* The Center for Philanthropy at Indiana University, 2012.

Giving USA. *Giving USA 2013 Annual Report.* The Center for Philanthropy at Indiana University, 2013.

Hammack, David C. *Making The Nonprofit Sector in the United States: A Reader.* Bloomington and Indianapolis: Indiana University Press, 1998.

Harbaugh, William T. et al, Neural Responses to Taxation and Voluntary Giving Reveal Motives for Charitable Donations, *Science* 15 June 2007:Vol. 316 no. 5831 pp. 1622-1625

Havens, John J. and Paul G. Schervish. "Why the $41 Trillion Wealth Transfer Estimate is Still Valid." Planning Giving Design Center Network. www.pgdc.com/print/29102.

LeMay, Kathy. *The Generosity Plan: Sharing Your Time, Treasure and Talent to Shape the World.* New York: Atria, 2009.

Lyubomirsky, Sonja. *The How of Happiness: A New Approach to Getting the Life You Want.* New York: Penguin Books, 2008.

McCarty, Oseola. *Simple Wisdom For Rich Living.* Atlanta: Longstreet Press, 1996.

Payton, Robert L. and Michael P. Moody. *Understanding Philanthropy: Its Meaning and Mission.* Bloomington and Indianapolis: Indiana University Press, 2008.

Sharpe Sr., Robert F. *Planned Giving Simplified: The Gift, the Giver, and the Gift Planner.* John Wiley & Sons., 1999.

Smith, Wendy. *Give A Little: How Your Small Donations Can Transform Our World.* New York: Hyperion, 2009.

"Philanthropy." *The New Lexicon Webster's Dictionary of the English Language.* Encyclopedic Edition. New York: Lexicon Publishers, Inc, 1989.

Tierney, Thomas J. and Joel L. Fleishman. *Give Smart: Philanthropy That Gets Results.* New York: Public Affairs, 2012.

Endnotes

[i] Payton, Robert L. and Michael P. Moody, *Understanding Philanthropy: Its Meaning and Mission* (Bloomington and Indianapolis: Indiana University Press, 2008), 13-14, 63.

[ii] "Philanthropy," *The New Lexicon Webster's Dictionary of the English Language,* Encyclopedic Edition (New York: Lexicon Pubishers, Inc, 1989), 754.

[iii] Payton & Moody.

[iv] Payton & Moody, 7.

[v] McCarty, Oseola., *Simple Wisdom For Rich Living* (Atlanta: Longstreet Press, 1996), xii-xiii.

[vi] Giving USA, *Giving USA 2013 Annual Report,* (The Center for Philanthropy at Indiana University, 2013), 12-13.

[vii] Neural Responses to Taxation and Voluntary Giving Reveal Motives for Charitable Donations, William T. Harbaugh, Ulrich Mayr, Daniel R. Burghart1, *Science* 15 June 2007:Vol. 316 no. 5831 pp. 1622-1625

[viii] Lyubomirsky, Sonja, *The How of Happiness: A New Approach to Getting the Life You Want* (New York: Penguin Books, 2008), 88-124.

[ix] Lyubomirsky, 90.

[x] Lyubomirsky, 90.

[xi] Lyubomirsky, 92-95.

[xii] Payton & Moody, 15.

[xiii] Payton & Moody, 15.

[xiv] Havens, John J. and Paul G. Schervish, "Why the $41 Trillion Wealth Transfer Estimate is Still Valid," Planning Giv-

ing Design Center Network, www.pgdc.com/print/29102.

[xv]Sharpe Sr., Robert F., *Planned Giving Simplified: The Gift, the Giver, and the Gift Planner* (John Wiley & Sons, 1999), 189.

[xvi]Arnsberger, Paul, et al. "A History of the Tax-Exempt Sector: An SOI Perspective." Internal Revenue Service, Winter 2007–2008, 106.

[xvii]Arnsberger, et al., 110.

[xviii]LeMay, Kathy, *The Generosity Plan: Sharing Your Time, Treasure and Talent to Shape the World* (New York: Atria, 2009), 74.

[xix]Giving USA, *Giving USA 2012 Annual Report,* 51.

[xx]LeMay, 1.

[xxi]Le May, 18.

[xxii]Giving USA, *Giving USA 2012 Annual Report.*

[xxiii]Federal Trade Commission, "Consumer Information: Before Giving to a Charity," June 2012, http://www.consumer. ftc.gov/articles/0074-giving-charity.

[xxiv]LeMay, 82-83.

[xxv]*McDonald & Co. Sec., Inc., Gradison Div. v. Alzheimer's Disease & Related Disorders Assn., Inc.,* 140 Ohio App. 3d 358, 361, 747 N.E.2d 843, 846 (2000).

[xxvi]Lyubomirsky, 132.

[xxvii]Arnold, Elizabeth, *Creating the Good Will: The Most Comprehensive Guide to Both the Financial AND Emotional Sides of Passing On Your Legacy* (New York: Penguin Group, 2005), 4-5.

CPSIA information can be obtained at www.ICGtesting.com
Printed in the USA
LVOW04s2146131114

413644LV00014B/431/P